Super Science
Stuck On Magnets

by Kate Mason

Copyright © 1995 by Watermill Press,
an imprint of Troll Associates, Inc.

Printed in the United States of America.

ISBN 0-8167-3670-7
10 9 8 7 6 5 4 3 2 1

Contents

Super Science
Stuck On Magnets

Introduction

At this moment you are living on a giant magnet. This giant magnet is called Earth. The force that comes from this giant magnet is called *magnetism*. It is one of the most important forces in nature. Without magnetism there would be no motors, video games, or television.

Super Science Stuck On Magnets shows you how magnetism powers everything from telephones to space shuttles. There are even fun magnet experiments for you and your friends to do. This great kit includes the components you'll need to explore the exciting world of magnetism:

- **2 square magnets**
- **2 bar magnets**
- **copper wire**
- **steel rod**
- **wooden dowel**
- **plastic foam base**

Some other materials you will need for your experiments, like paper clips, tape, markers or crayons, and construction paper, can be found around your house or at a craft store.

Tips

1. Good scientists always set up their labs first. Make sure that you have gathered all the materials you will need to complete each experiment before you begin. And remember, some science experiments will require a grown-up helper.

2. If your experiment doesn't work the first time, try it again. Don't worry if your results aren't exactly the same as those in this book. Try to figure out what happened and why.

3. Keep a notebook close by to write down the conclusions of your experiments. This way you can compare the results of each experiment. Who knows... maybe you will come across a new scientific discovery!

What Makes a Magnet a Magnet?

A **magnet** is a piece of iron, steel or other metal that can *attract*, or pull closer, other pieces of iron or steel. Iron is made of tiny particles called *atoms*. Whether or not a metal is a magnet depends on how its atoms are arranged. If you could see the atoms inside an ordinary nail, you would see that they are all scattered and disorganized.

If you could see the atoms inside a magnetized nail, you would notice that they are organized and they all face in the same direction.

Scattered Atoms

Ordinary Nail

Magnetized Nail

Organized Atoms

The Poles of a Magnet

A magnet's force is strongest at its ends. The ends of a magnet are called *poles*. One pole of the magnet is called the *north pole*. The other pole of the magnet is called the *south pole*. Later on, you'll find out which end of your bar magnet is north and which end is south by creating a working compass.

South Pole ——→   ←—— **North Pole**

The poles of a magnet do most of the magnet's work. They are the muscle behind its pulling power. What do you think would happen if the powerful poles of two magnets got near each other? Here's where the fun starts. If a pole of one magnet is brought near a pole of another magnet, they will either attract or *repel* each other.

4

Poles That Attract and Repel

If you hold a magnet in each hand and try to press two opposite poles together (north and south) they will attract.

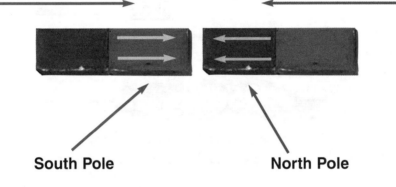

South Pole   **North Pole**

If opposite poles attract, what do you think will happen if you try to press two identical poles together? If you try to press the north pole of each magnet together, they will repel, or push apart. The same thing will happen if you try to press the south poles together.

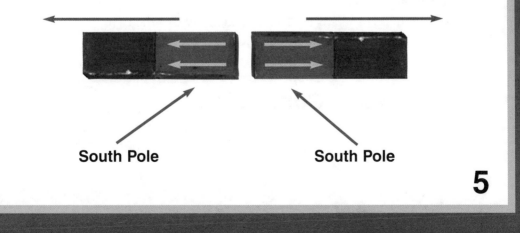

South Pole   **South Pole**

Q: If two magnets are pressed together, which of their poles will attract and which of their poles will repel?

Experiment #1
Incredible Floating Magnets

Prepare your lab:

- two square magnets
- plastic foam base
- dowel rod

Steps

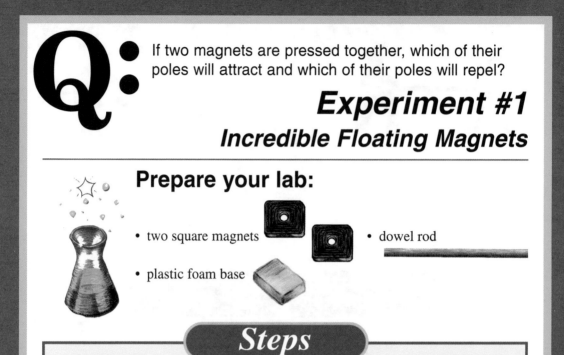

1. Set the plastic foam base on a table. Place the dowel rod in the top of the plastic foam base so that the dowel rod stands straight up.

2. Slip one of the magnets onto the dowel rod and let it fall to the bottom.

3. Slip the second magnet onto the dowel.

4. Watch what they do. If they snap together, you know that the north pole of one magnet is touching the south pole of the other magnet. But if the top magnet seems to "float," you know that the two poles facing each other are identical. They are either two north poles or two south poles.

Conclusion:
Two magnets' opposite poles attract and two magnets' identical poles repel.

The Magical Magnetic Field

Here's a fun fact about magnets: A magnet's north and south poles line up with Earth's north and south poles. The reason for this is because Earth is also a giant magnet. And all magnets, including Earth, are surrounded by an invisible force called a **magnetic field**.

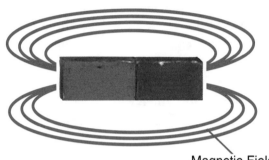

Magnetic Field

A magnetic field reaches out into the space around the magnet. This is what creates the "strength" of a magnet.

It's easy to see a magnetic field in action. All you have to do is put a magnet on a table and cover the magnet with a sheet of paper. Then sprinkle iron filings over the paper. Wait and watch as the filings line up with the strength of the magnetic field. The filings will be more crowded where the magnetic field is strongest, which is at the magnet's poles.

If you don't have iron filings, you could cut up some steel wool pads instead. Be very careful when cutting steel wool pads. To protect your hands, be sure to wear gloves when cutting or handling iron filings or steel wool.

Where the magnetic field is the **strongest**

Where the magnetic field is the **weakest**

Magnets From Earth

Earth's huge magnetic field is believed to be created by extremely hot molten iron deep in the center of Earth. As Earth spins, this hot molten iron also spins and creates electrical currents.

These electric currents cause Earth to act like there's a giant invisible bar magnet in its center with its own magnetic north pole and its own magnetic south pole. Look at the illustration below. Earth's magnetic north pole and magnetic south pole are named for the poles they attract. We know that opposites attract. Therefore Earth's magnetic north pole is the south pole of the invisible bar magnet, and Earth's magnetic south pole is the north pole of the invisible bar magnet.

Earth's magnetic north pole is really 870 miles (1,400 km) away from the geographic North Pole. Earth's magnetic south pole is really 1,710 miles (2,753 km) away from the geographic South Pole.

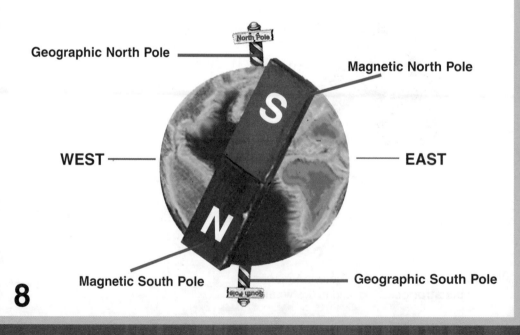

Magnetite, Solids, and Other Minerals

Because Earth is a giant magnet and has such a powerful magnetic field, it produces natural magnetic rocks. The ancient Greeks found many magnetic rocks in a place called Magnesia which is now the country of Turkey. This type of rock was named **magnetite**, and anything that acts like it is called a magnet.

Magnetite is a strange and wonderful magnetic rock that can pick up pieces of iron. It is hard and black. Magnetite is found all over the world, and large deposits of magnetite have been found in New York, Vermont, Utah, California, and New Mexico.

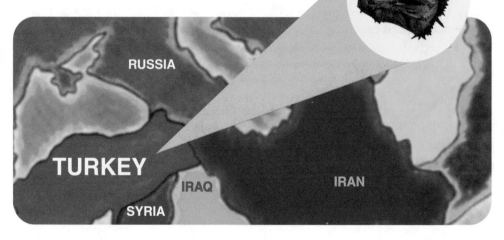

Besides magnetite, Earth also produces minerals like iron and cobalt. Iron and cobalt can also be made into **permanent magnets**. Permanent magnets are magnetized all the time.

You know that Earth's magnetic field is a very powerful natural force that can travel through air. But did you know that it can also travel through solids? The next experiment will prove this.

9

Q: Is a magnet's magnetic field strong enough to travel through solids?

Experiment #2
Super Speedway

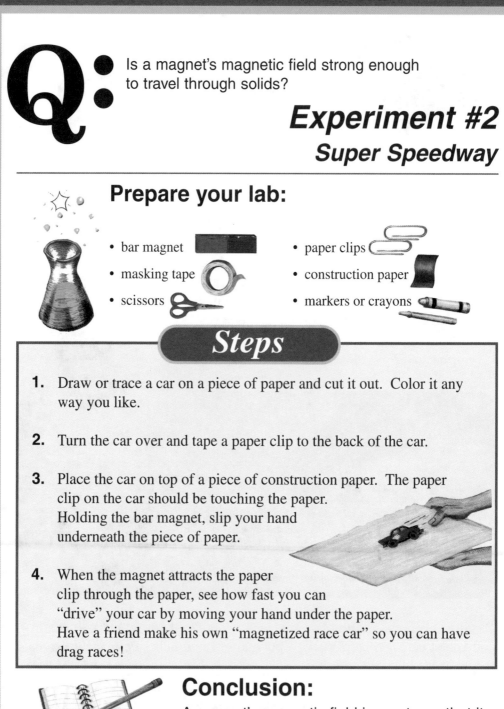

Prepare your lab:

- bar magnet
- masking tape
- scissors
- paper clips
- construction paper
- markers or crayons

Steps

1. Draw or trace a car on a piece of paper and cut it out. Color it any way you like.

2. Turn the car over and tape a paper clip to the back of the car.

3. Place the car on top of a piece of construction paper. The paper clip on the car should be touching the paper. Holding the bar magnet, slip your hand underneath the piece of paper.

4. When the magnet attracts the paper clip through the paper, see how fast you can "drive" your car by moving your hand under the paper. Have a friend make his own "magnetized race car" so you can have drag races!

Conclusion:

A magnet's magnetic field is so strong that it can travel through solids.

The Compass

An airplane pilot uses one. A ship's captain uses one. If you were lost in a desert, you might walk in circles unless you had one. We're talking about a compass.

Compasses have changed the way people live. They have guided people around the world, opened the world to trade, and helped people learn about other countries. Where did these amazing instruments come from?

Around A.D. 1200, Europeans discovered that a long, thin piece of magnetite always pointed north and south when it was hung on a string. Europeans used this as the first compass and gave magnetite the special name *lodestone*, which means "the stone that leads."

How Does a Compass Work?

A compass has a pointer, or needle, in it. This needle is magnetized and can turn freely. No matter how much you move the compass around, the magnetic needle will always point north and south. The next experiment will show you how to make your own simple compass.

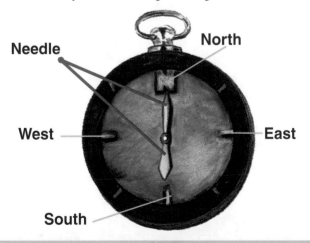

Needle

North

West

East

South

11

Q: How can a magnet become a compass?

Experiment #3
Let Your Magnet Point the Way

Prepare your lab:

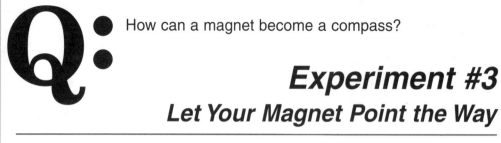

- bar magnet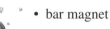
- masking tape
- 12-inch (30.5-cm) piece of string

- ruler
- a small piece of paper
- heavy books

Steps

1. Wrap the string around the middle of the bar magnet and tie a knot.

2. Tie the other end of the string to one end of a ruler.

3. Place the other end of the ruler on the edge of a table and stack some heavy books on top of it to hold the ruler in place. The magnet should be hanging off the table and swinging.

4. When the magnet stops swinging, it will be facing north and south. Mark a tiny piece of paper with an "N" and tape it to the end of the magnet pointing north. If you're not sure which end of the magnet is pointing north, ask a grown-up to show you.

Conclusion:

By using your magnet to find which way is north, you have created a simple compass.

Q: How can you magnetize a needle to make a real working magnet?

Experiment #4
Make a Magnet for Your Compass

Prepare your lab:

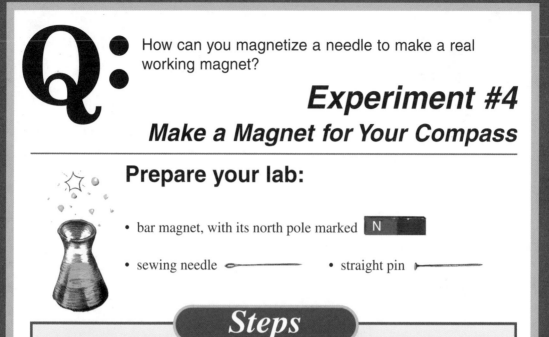

- bar magnet, with its north pole marked

- sewing needle

- straight pin

Steps

1. Hold the rounded end, or eye, of the needle in one hand and the magnet in the other hand. **Be very careful to hold the point of the needle away from you!**

2. Starting at the end of the needle closest to your hand, begin rubbing the north pole of the magnet along the needle. Rub in one direction only. Do not go back and forth! Rub the needle about 50 times. This action will force the atoms in the needle to temporarily line up and face in the same direction.

3. Touch the tip of the needle to the straight pin. Did the needle pick up the straight pin? Great! You've just magnetized your needle!

Conclusion:

You can magnetize a needle by making its atoms line up in the same direction. Now that your sewing needle is magnetized, you have half of your working compass.

Q: Why is a magnetized needle used to make a real working compass?

Experiment #5
Making a Working Compass

Prepare your lab:

- thin piece of cork or plastic foam
- your magnetized needle

- bowl of water
- glue or tape

Steps

1. Attach the magnetized needle to the cork or plastic foam by gluing or taping the needle to one side of the cork or plastic foam.

2. Fill a small bowl halfway with water and float the cork or plastic foam in the water with the magnetized needle facing up.

3. Wait until the needle stops spinning. When it does, it will be pointing north. Try turning the bowl. The needle will still point in the same direction.

Believe it or not, the compass you've just created could help you find your way around the world. Once you know which way is north, you would then know that east is to your right, west is on your left, and south is behind you.

Conclusion:
A magnetized needle is used to make a real working compass because a magnetized needle will always point north.

The Transfer of Magnetism

We know that an iron nail is not a magnet. It will not pick up another nail. But a fascinating thing happens when you pick up a nail with a permanent magnet. The magnetism from the magnet lines up the atoms in the nail.

If you lower the tip of the nail over a second nail, it will pick it up! If you lower the tip of the second nail over a third nail, it will also pick it up. But if you move the magnet away from the first nail, then the "chain of magnetism" will be broken. All three nails will lose their magnetism and fall.

The magnetism only lasts as long as the first nail is attached to a magnet. These nails are called **temporary magnets**.

The next experiment shows you how to create a magnetic paper clip chain by transferring magnetism. This will be fun!

Q: If a permanent magnet transfers its magnetism to an object, is that object then a permanent magnet?

Experiment #6
The Magnetic Chain

Prepare your lab:

- bar magnet
- paper clips

Steps

1. Gather some paper clips and lay them in a line on a table. Be sure to unlink any of the paper clips that may be joined together.

2. Touch the magnet to one paper clip. Remember that as the magnet holds the paper clip, the paper clip is becoming temporarily magnetized.

3. Lower the magnet and magnetized paper clip until it touches another paper clip. Make sure the magnet touches only one paper clip.

4. Slowly lift the magnet up again. What happened? You should have another paper clip hanging from the first one. See how many paper clips you can pick up to make a chain.

Conclusion:

The paper clips in your paper clip chain are temporary magnets. These temporary magnets are only magnetized as long as they are attached to a permanent magnet.

Magnetism and Electricity

You know that Earth creates natural magnets and the metals to make permanent magnets. Remember that a permanent magnet keeps its magnetism all the time. You used a permanent magnet to magnetize the needle of your compass. Now it's time to learn about temporary magnets.

The ability to create temporary magnets is one of the most important and exciting parts of magnetism. The most fascinating type of temporary magnet is called an **electromagnet**.

MAGNETISM AND ELECTRICITY
There is a very special relationship between magnetism and electricity. These two forces cannot be separated. Electricity creates a special kind of temporary magnetism called *electromagnetism.*

THE AMAZING ELECTROMAGNET
An electromagnet is a magnet that is created by using an electric current. An electromagnet can be made with a coil of wire, a nail, and a battery. The nail becomes magnetized when an electric current flows through the wire. Just like a lamp, an electromagnet can be switched on and off.

USES FOR AN ELECTROMAGNET
You may not realize it, but we use electromagnets every day for many different reasons. If there were no electromagnets, there would be no televisions, telephones, or radios. There would be no electric motors to run our hair dryers, fans, and many of our appliances. Can you imagine how many magnets are at work inside a space shuttle?

HOW DOES AN ELECTROMAGNET WORK?
An electromagnet is connected to a source of electricity, such as a battery. The battery produces an electric current. Whenever an electric current flows through a wire, a magnetic field is created around the wire. When the wire is wrapped around a nail, the atoms in the nail line up. When this happens, the nail becomes a magnet!

17

Q:

Why can't electricity and magnetism be separated?

Experiment #7
Make an Electromagnet

Prepare your lab:

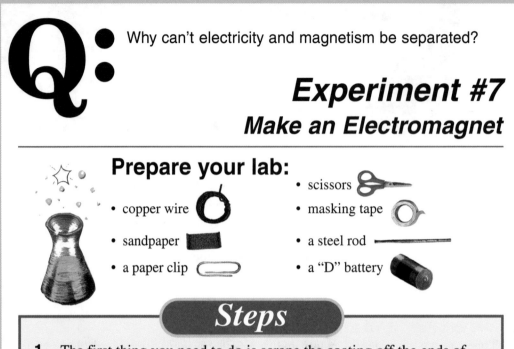

- copper wire
- sandpaper
- a paper clip

- scissors
- masking tape
- a steel rod
- a "D" battery

Steps

1. The first thing you need to do is scrape the coating off the ends of your piece of wire. Take your sandpaper in one hand and one end of the wire in the other hand. Fold the sandpaper around the end of the wire and gently sand the end until the coating is completely off. Repeat this step for the other end of the wire.

2. Now pick up the wire in one hand and the steel rod in the other. Leave 7 inches (17.8 cm) of wire free before you start wrapping. Starting at one end of the rod, wrap the wire around the rod 50 or 60 times. Wrap the wire neatly and tightly, always going in the same direction. Leave an extra 7 inches (17.8 cm) of wire and cut the rest off.

3. Place one end of the wire on the end of the battery with the raised tip. Use a piece of masking tape to hold the wire to the end of the battery. Try to pick up the paper clip with the end of the steel rod. It won't work.

18

4. Take the other end of the wire and put it on the opposite end of the battery. Use a piece of masking tape to hold it in place. Believe it or not, you've just made an electromagnet. Let's try it!

Touch the end of the rod to a paper clip. What happened this time? It picked the clip up!

WARNING!

Do not leave the wire attached to the battery for more than two minutes! The electric current running through the wire can make the wire very hot!

If your electromagnet did not work, don't worry. The reason is probably very simple. Check your wire connections. One of the ends of the wire probably isn't firmly taped to the battery. Remember that many famous scientific discoveries started out as simple mistakes.

Conclusion:

When an electric current flows through a wire, a magnetic field is automatically created around the wire. Therefore, electricity and magnetism cannot be separated.

19

Superconductors

You've seen for yourself how important magnets are in our everyday lives. From ancient lodestones to electromagnets, magnetism has inspired scientists to invent many important machines and appliances.

But it doesn't stop there. Scientists are already experimenting with **superconductors**. These magnets are more powerful than electromagnets, and use much less electricity. A superconducting magnetic disc has such a strong magnetic field around it that a solid cobalt ball will actually *float* above it! Superconductors are the magnets of the future.

Using superconductors, Japanese researchers have already created a train called a *maglev* (magnetic levitation). The maglev train really floats above the train tracks. Friction between an ordinary train and the train tracks keeps the train from going very fast. Since the maglev floats above the tracks, there is no friction between the train and the tracks, so the maglev can travel at very high speeds. Maglev trains will eventually be able to travel at speeds of more than 300 miles (480 km) per hour.

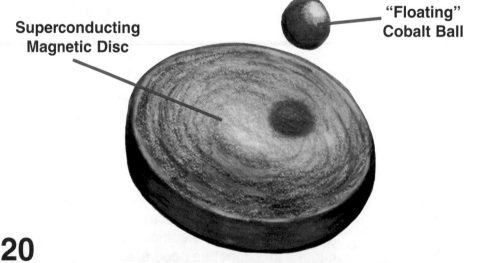

"Floating"
Cobalt Ball

Superconducting
Magnetic Disc

Q: How can you "demagnetize" a magnet?

Experiment #8
"Breaking" a Magnet

Prepare your lab:

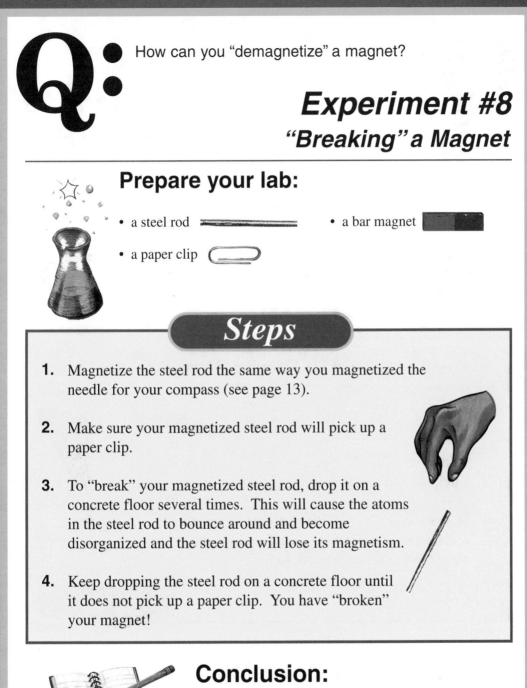

- a steel rod
- a bar magnet
- a paper clip

Steps

1. Magnetize the steel rod the same way you magnetized the needle for your compass (see page 13).

2. Make sure your magnetized steel rod will pick up a paper clip.

3. To "break" your magnetized steel rod, drop it on a concrete floor several times. This will cause the atoms in the steel rod to bounce around and become disorganized and the steel rod will lose its magnetism.

4. Keep dropping the steel rod on a concrete floor until it does not pick up a paper clip. You have "broken" your magnet!

Conclusion:

You can demagnetize a magnet by causing its atoms to become disorganized.

Q: You've learned that magnetism can pass through solids. Can magnetism also fly through the air?

Experiment #9
Flying High

Prepare your lab:

- construction paper
- scissors
- masking tape
- a paper clip
- two square magnets
- thread

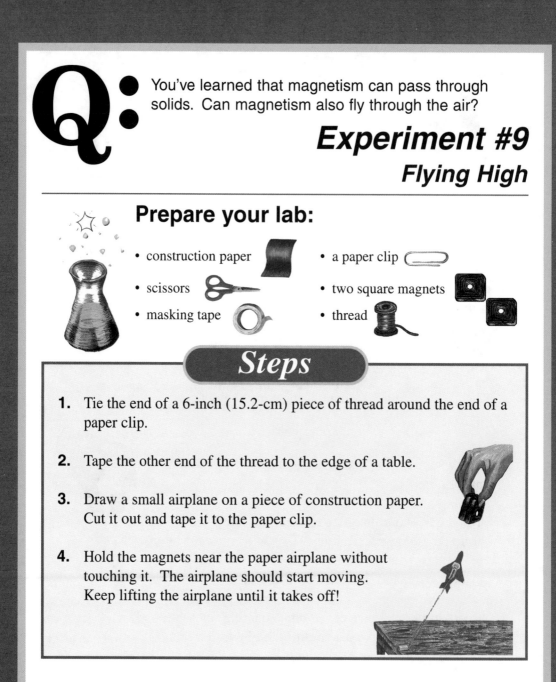

Steps

1. Tie the end of a 6-inch (15.2-cm) piece of thread around the end of a paper clip.

2. Tape the other end of the thread to the edge of a table.

3. Draw a small airplane on a piece of construction paper. Cut it out and tape it to the paper clip.

4. Hold the magnets near the paper airplane without touching it. The airplane should start moving. Keep lifting the airplane until it takes off!

Conclusion:
A magnet's magnetic field is so strong that it can "fly" through the air.

Q: You've proven that magnetism can pass through solids and the air. Can magnetism pass through water?

Experiment #10
Anchors Away!

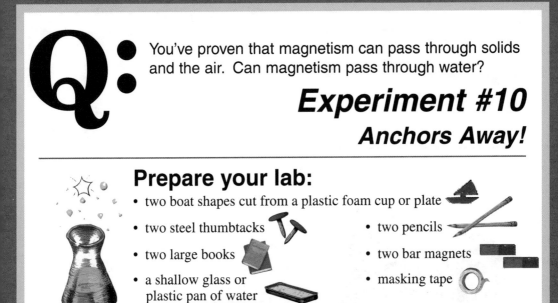

Prepare your lab:

- two boat shapes cut from a plastic foam cup or plate
- two steel thumbtacks
- two large books
- a shallow glass or plastic pan of water
- two pencils
- two bar magnets
- masking tape

Steps

You may want to have a friend help you with this experiment.

1. Place the books on a table about six inches (15 cm) apart. Place the pan filled with shallow water across the books.

2. Tape a magnet to one end of each pencil.

3. Push a tack through the middle of each boat. Float the boats in the water, with their tack sides facing the water.

4. You and your friend stand on opposite sides of the pan. Each of you holds a pencil under the pan and races your boats by moving the magnets. As the magnets move, so will the boats!

Conclusion:

A magnet's magnetic field is so strong that it can pass through water.

Magnetism and You

Through simple experiments, you've seen that a magnet is much more than a toy or something that holds a note to your refrigerator. Magnets supply the power for many of the things we do, from blow-drying our hair to ringing a doorbell. You've learned what a magnetic field is, how magnetism can be transferred from one object to another, and about the important relationship between magnetism and electricity.

There's a magnet at work inside a hair dryer.

Now that you know all about magnets, it's time to look for examples of magnetism in and around your house. You can even make up new experiments to see how these different types of magnetism work. Don't worry if you don't understand all the things you see. You might be discovering something new. You could become one of the great scientists of the future.

Magnets hold notes to your refrigerator.

The microphone, the speaker, and the bell inside a telephone all need magnetism to make them work.